French

Aladdin Books
Macmillan Publishing Company
New York

© 1989 by **BERLITZ PUBLICATIONS, INC.**, a Macmillan Company
866 Third Avenue, New York NY 10022

Aladdin Books
Macmillan Publishing Company
866 Third Avenue, New York, NY 10022
Collier Macmillan Canada, Inc.

First Aladdin Books edition 1989

Printed in Italy

ISBN 0-689-71312-6

Published as a world-wide co-edition in collaboration with
Dami Editore, Milano
Illustrations by Tony Wolf

Library of Congress Cataloging-in-Publication Data

Berlitz Jr. French — 1st Aladdin Books ed.
p. cm.
Summary: Teddy Berlitz introduces basic French phrases, the alphabet,
numbers, and colors. Accompanying cassette incorporates music, sound effects,
and voices of native speakers.
ISBN 0-689-71312-6

1. French language—Textbooks for foreign speakers—English—Juvenile
literature. 2. French language—Conversation and phrase
books—English—Juvenile literature. (1. French language—Textbooks for
foreign speakers—English. 2. French language—Conversation and phrase
books—English.) I. Berlitz Schools of Languages of America.
PC2129.E5J4 1989
448.2'4—dc19   88-37546
CIP
AC

To the parent:

Learning a foreign language is one of the best ways to expand a child's horizons. It immediately exposes him or her to a foreign culture—especially important in a time when the world is more of a "global village" than ever before.

Berlitz Jr. is the first Berlitz program of its kind. Like the adult language programs that Berlitz pioneered, the Berlitz Jr. teaching method is based on clear and simplified conversations, without the need for grammatical drills. Within minutes, just by listening to our sixty-minute cassette and following the beautifully illustrated text, your child will be saying a few simple but invaluable foreign phrases.

Your child will love Teddy and enjoy meeting his family and friends. Together you and your child can follow Teddy to school, where he learns how to count and spell, and then on to playtime in the park and a visit to the circus. All you have to do is listen and repeat. You will hear native speakers saying each phrase clearly. There is a long pause after each phrase so that your child can repeat it, imitating the authentic pronunciation. Music and sound effects add to the fun.

All the phrases on the cassette are found in the book, together with a translation, illustrated by lively and appealing drawings. And if you want to find the exact meaning of a word quickly, just look it up in the foreign-language vocabulary at the back of the book. The book and cassette reinforce each other but can be used separately once your child is comfortable with them.

All children have the potential to speak a foreign language. By using frequently repeated words in a storybook form, Teddy Berlitz allows children to tap that potential. These carefully constructed texts have been approved by school language-experts and meet the Berlitz standard of quality. Best of all, the book-cassette format enables a new language to be learned in much the same way your child first learned to speak.

Enjoy sharing Teddy Berlitz—and watching your child's world grow.

Berlitz Publications

Voici Teddy!
Here's Teddy!

Bonjour! Je m'appelle Teddy.
Hello! My name is Teddy.

Je suis un ours.
I am a bear.

Je parle français.
I speak French.

Et toi? Est-ce que tu parles français?
And you? Do you speak French?

Oui
Yes

Non
No

Non, je ne parle pas français.
No, I don't speak French.

Est-ce que tu parles anglais?
Do you speak English?

Oui  Non
Yes *No*

Oui, je parle anglais.
Yes, I speak English.

Moi, je m'appelle Teddy.
My name is Teddy.

Et toi, comment t'appelles-tu?
And you? What's your name?

Pardon? Comment t'appelles-tu?
Excuse me? What's your name?

Je m'appelle...
My name is ...

Merci!
Thank you!

Voici ma maison.
This is my house.

Ma maison est dans la forêt.
My house is in the forest.

Ma maison est petite. Elle n'est pas grande.
My house is little. It isn't big.

Il y a beaucoup d'arbres et de fleurs dans la forêt.
There are many trees and flowers in the forest.

C'est une belle forêt.
It's a beautiful forest.

Voici mon papa.
This is my daddy.

Voici ma maman.
This is my mommy.

J'aime mon papa.
I love my daddy.

J'aime ma maman.
I love my mommy.

J'aime mes parents.
I love my parents.

Mes parents disent bonjour.
My parents say hello.

J'ai une soeur.
I have a sister.

J'ai un frère.
I have a brother.

Mon frère s'appelle Pierre.
My brother's name is Pierre.

Ma soeur s'appelle Marie.
My sister's name is Marie.

Je suis grand.
I am big.

Pierre et Marie sont petits.
Pierre and Marie are little.

Ce sont des bébés!
They are babies!

Pierre, Marie et moi, nous avons beaucoup de jouets.
Pierre, Marie, and I have a lot of toys.

Nous avons:
We have:

un train,
a train,

un ballon,
a ball,

une poupée,
a doll,

une voiture,
a car,

un avion,
a plane,

un bateau,
a boat,

un seau et une pelle.
a pail, and a shovel.

Nous aimons jouer avec les jouets.
We like to play with the toys.

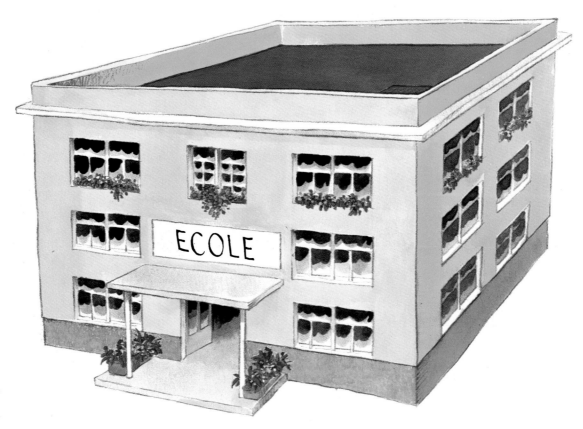

Voici mon école.
This is my school.

Mon école est en ville.
My school is in the town.

Je vais à l'école le lundi, le mardi,
le mercredi, le jeudi et le vendredi.
I go to school on Monday, Tuesday, Wednesday,
Thursday, and Friday.

6 SAMEDI

7 DIMANCHE

Je ne vais pas à l'école le samedi et le dimanche.
I don't go to school on Saturday and Sunday.

**1
LUNDI**

Aujourd'hui c'est lundi. Je vais à l'école.
Today is Monday. I am going to school.

Voici ma classe.
This is my classroom.

Voici la maîtresse.
This is the teacher.

Bonjour, je suis Madame Duval.
Hello, I am Madame Duval.

Dites bonjour à Madame Duval!
Say hello to Madame Duval!

Bonjour!
Hello!

Voici Gigi.
This is Gigi.

Bonjour.
Hello.

Est-ce que Gigi est la maîtresse?
Is Gigi the teacher?

Non, Gigi n'est pas la maîtresse.
No, Gigi is not the teacher.

Gigi n'est pas Madame Duval.
Gigi is not Madame Duval.

Gigi est une élève!
Gigi is a student!

Gigi lit les numéros.
Gigi is reading the numbers.

Un, deux, trois, quatre, cinq, six, sept, huit, neuf, dix.
One, two, three, four, five, six, seven, eight, nine, ten.

Compte avec nous de un à dix.
Let's count from one to ten.

Est-ce que tu peux compter avec Gigi?
Can you count with Gigi?

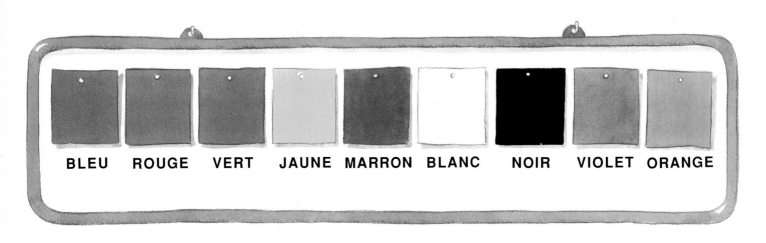

| BLEU | ROUGE | VERT | JAUNE | MARRON | BLANC | NOIR | VIOLET | ORANGE |

Voici Henri.   Henri joue avec les couleurs.
This is Henri.   *Henri is playing with the colors.*

Bleu, rouge, vert, jaune, marron, blanc, noir, violet, orange.
Blue, red, green, yellow, brown, white, black, purple, orange.

Moi, je sais écrire.
I know how to write.

J'écris A, B, C...
I'm writing A, B, C...

Regarde! J'écris l'alphabet: A, B, C, D, E...
Look! I'm writing the alphabet: A, B, C, D, E...

Maintenant je lis l'alphabet:
Now I'm reading the alphabet:

A, B, C, D, E, F, G, H, I, J, K, L, M,
N, O, P, Q, R, S, T, U, V, W, X, Y, Z.

J'épelle mon nom: T-E-D-D-Y.
I'm spelling my name: T-E-D-D-Y.

Teddy! C'est moi.
Teddy! That's me.

Et toi? Est-ce que tu peux épeler ton nom?
And you? Can you spell your name?

Nous chantons à l'école.
We sing at school.

Voici une chanson.
Here's a song.

Et toi? Est-ce que tu chantes avec nous?
And you? Will you sing with us?

Chante avec nous!
Come on, sing with us!

Calmez-vous, les enfants.
Un... deux... trois...
Quiet, children.
One... two... three...

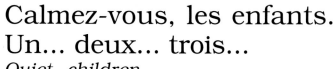

ABCDEFG
HIJKLMNOP
QRS TUV W
XYZ.

J'ai chanté mon ABC.
I have sung my ABC.

Dites-moi si ça vous plaît.
Tell me if you like it.

Bien! Très bien!
Good! Very good!

Toute la classe: quelle heure est-il?
Class: what time is it?

Il est trois heures!
It's three o'clock!

Est-ce qu'il est une heure? Non.
Is it one o'clock? No.

Est-ce qu'il est deux heures?
Is it two o'clock?

Non. Il est trois heures! Bravo!
No. It's three o'clock! Yaay!

L'école est finie.
School is over.

Au revoir, Madame Duval!
Good-bye, Madame Duval!

ECOLE

Au revoir, Teddy!
Good-bye, Teddy!

Au revoir, Gigi!
Good-bye, Gigi!

Au revoir, Henri!
Good-bye, Henri!

La Surprise

The Surprise

Allons tous au parc de jeux.
Let's all go to the playground.

Le parc de jeux est près de l'école.
The playground is near the school.

Il y a beaucoup de choses à faire au parc de jeux.
There are a lot of things to do in the playground.

Je suis sur la balançoire!
I'm on the swing!

Je descends le toboggan.
I'm going down the slide.

Allons tous sur le manège.
Let's all go on the merry-go-round.

A quatre heures nous rentrons à la maison.
At four o'clock we all go home.

Je marche vers la forêt.
I walk to the forest.

Je marche sur le chemin.
I walk on the road.

Il y a une affiche sur un arbre.
There is a poster on a tree.

Sur l'affiche je lis: "Cirque".
On the poster I read: "Circus".

C'est amusant!
That's fun!

Quelle surprise à la maison!
And when I get home — surprise!

Teddy, est-ce que tu veux aller au cirque?
Teddy, would you like to go to the circus?

Au cirque? Oh, oui, oui! Allons-y!
To the circus? Oh, yes, yes! Let's go!

Samedi maman m'emmène au cirque.
On Saturday Mommy takes me to the circus.

Pierre et Marie restent à la maison avec papa.
Pierre and Marie stay at home with Daddy.

Le cirque est près du parc.
The circus is near the park.

La tente du cirque est rouge et bleue.
The circus tent is red and blue.

Tout le monde fait la queue.
Everybody is standing in line.

Bonjour, je m'appelle Julie.
Hello, my name is Julie.

Je m'appelle Teddy.
My name is Teddy.

Voici mon frère Paul.
This is my brother Paul.

Asseyons-nous ensemble.
Let's all sit together.

Est-ce qu'il y a des crocodiles au cirque?
Are there crocodiles in the circus?

Non, mais il y a des lions.
No, but there are lions.

Est-ce qu'il y a des girafes au cirque?
Are there giraffes in the circus?

Non, mais il y a des zèbres.
No, but there are zebras.

Il y a des singes au cirque.
There are monkeys in the circus.

Combien de singes?
How many monkeys?

Je ne sais pas. Comptons: un, deux,
I don't know. Let's count: one, two,

trois, quatre, cinq, six. Six singes.
three, four, five, six. Six monkeys.

Voici un éléphant. Comme il est grand!
Here's an elephant. How big he is!

Regarde, deux clowns!
Look, two clowns!

L'un est heureux, l'autre est triste.
One is happy, the other is sad.

Voici la parade! C'est une grande parade!
Here's the parade! It's a big parade!

Regarde tous les animaux!
Look at all the animals!

Après le cirque nous achetons des glaces.
After the circus we buy ice cream.

Je voudrais une glace au chocolat.
I want chocolate ice cream.

Moi, je voudrais une glace à la fraise.
I want strawberry ice cream.

Pour moi à la vanille.
I'll have vanilla.

Paul, où est-ce que tu habites?
Paul, where do you live?

J'habite près du parc de jeux.
I live near the playground.

Alors tu vas à l'école près d'ici?
So you go to school near here?

Oui.
Yes.

On peut jouer ensemble après l'école.
Then we can play together after school.

Au revoir, Paul.
Good-bye, Paul.

Au revoir, Teddy.
Good-bye, Teddy.

Vocabulary

A

a—has
    il y a—there is/are
à—at, to
    à l'école—at school
    Je vais à l'école.—I go to school.
achetons—(we) buy
affiche—poster
ai—(I) have
    J'ai un frère.—I have a brother.
aime—(I) love
aimons—(we) love
    Nous aimons jouer avec les jouets.
    We like to play with the toys.
aller—to go
allons—(we) go
    Allons-y!—Let's go!
alors—so
    Alors tu vas à l'école près d'ici?
    So you go to school near here?
alphabet—alphabet
amusant—fun
    C'est amusant!—That's fun!
anglais—English
animaux—animals
appelle, appelles—call (name)
    Je m'appelle Teddy.
    My name is Teddy.
    Mon frère s'appelle Pierre.
    My brother's name is Pierre.
    Comment t'appelles-tu?
    What's your name?
après—after
    après l'école—after school
arbre(s)—tree(s)
asseyons-nous—let's sit (down)
au—in, to
    au cirque—in the circus
    aller au cirque— to go to the circus
    au revoir—good-bye
aujourd'hui—today
autre—other
    L'un est heureux, l'autre est triste.
    One is happy, the other is sad.
avec—with
avion—plane
avons—(we) have
    Nous avons une poupée.
    We have a doll.

B

balançoire—swing
    Je suis sur la balançoire!
    I'm on the swing!
ballon—ball
bateau—boat
beaucoup—a lot, many
    beaucoup de jouets—a lot of toys
    beaucoup d'arbres—many trees
bébés—babies
belle—beautiful
    une belle forêt—a beautiful forest
Bien!—Good!
blanc—white
bleu(e)—blue
Bonjour!—Hello!

C

c'—see **ce**
ça—that, it
calmez-vous—be quiet
    Calmez-vous, les enfants.
    Quiet, children.
ce, c'—that, it
    C'est moi.—That's me.
    C'est une grande parade!
    It's a big parade!
chanson—song
Chante!—Sing!
chanté—sung
    J'ai chanté mon ABC.
    I have sung my ABC.
chantes—(you) sing
chantons—(we) sing
    Nous chantons à l'école.
    We sing at school.
chemin—path, road
    Je marche sur le chemin.
    I walk on the road.
chocolat—chocolate
choses—things
cinq—five
cirque—circus
classe—class, classroom
clowns—clowns
combien—how many
comme—how
    Comme il est grand!—How big he is!

comment—how
  Comment t'appelles-tu?
  What's your name?
compter—to count
  Comptons!—Let's count!
couleurs—colors
crocodiles—crocodiles

D

d'—see **de**
dans—in
de, des, du, d'
  de un à dix—from one to ten
  beaucoup de choses—a lot of things
  Ce sont des bébés!— They are babies!
  près du parc—near the park
  près d'ici—near here
descends—(I) go down
deux—two
dimanche—Sunday
disent—(they) say
  Mes parents disent bonjour.
  My parents say hello.
dites-moi—tell me
dix—ten
du—see **de**

E

école—school
écrire—to write
écris—(I) write
  J'écris l'alphabet.
  I write the alphabet.
éléphant—elephant
élève—student
elle—she, it
emmène—(he/she) takes
  Maman m'emmène au cirque.
  Mommy takes me to the circus.
en—in
enfants—children
ensemble—together
épeler—to spell
épelle—(I) spell
  J'épelle mon nom.
  I'm spelling my name.
est—is
  c'est—it's, that's
Est-ce que...?—Is it...?
  Est-ce qu'il est une heure?
  Is it one o' clock?
  Est-ce que tu parles français?
  Do you speak French?

...est-il?—...is it?
  Quelle heure est-il?
  What time is it?
et—and

F

faire— to do
fait— does
  Tout le monde fait la queue.
  Everybody is standing in line.
finie— finished
  L'école est finie.—School is over.
fleurs—flowers
forêt—forest
fraise—strawberry
français—French
frère—brother

G

girafes—giraffes
glace(s)—ice cream
  glace au chocolat—chocolate ice cream
  glace à la fraise—strawberry ice cream
  Nous achetons des glaces.
  We buy ice cream.
grand(e)—big

H

habite—(I) live
  J'habite près du parc de jeux.
  I live near the playground.
habites—(you) live
heure(s)—hour(s), time
  Quelle heure est-il?
  What time is it?
  Il est trois heures!
  It's three o'clock!
heureux—happy
huit—eight

I

ici—here
il—he, it

J

jaune—yellow
je—I
jeudi—Thursday